NATURE
FORMS AND FORCES

PHOTOGRAPHS FROM OUR NATIONAL, STATE, AND LOCAL PARKS

ALGIMANTAS KEZYS

LOYOLA UNIVERSITY PRESS/CHICAGO

Published by

Loyola University Press
3441 North Ashland Avenue
Chicago, Illinois 60657

in cooperation with

The Midwest Museum of American Art
Elkhart, Indiana

Library of Congress Cataloging-in-Publication Data
Kezys, Algimantas. Nature, forms and forces.
Catalog of an exhibition held at Midwest Museum of American Art, 1985.
"Published . . . in cooperation with the Midwest Museum of American Art,
Elkhart, Indiana"—Copr. p.
1. Photography—Landscapes—Exhibitions.
2. Parks—United States—Pictorial Works—Exhibitions.
3. Kezys, Algimantas.
I. Midwest Museum of American Art (Elkhart, Ind.) II. Title.
TR660.K49 1986   779'.36'0924   86-2764
ISBN 0-8294-0525-9

CONTENTS

Introduction
vii

1   Water and Waterfalls
1

2   Patterns of the Earth
17

3   Enduring Stone
35

4   Sand Dunes and Seashores
51

5   Forms of Trees
67

6   Hot Springs of Yellowstone
95

List of Photographs
111

INTRODUCTION

It is often difficult to discern the forces which push the human spirit through time, through space. It is difficult to discern because of the variety of forces at work (physical, mental, man-made, natural, and so on) and the degree to which they act upon each of us individually. People have been able to adapt to change over thousands of years, responding to the forces which acted upon them at any given moment in their brief existences; and they have often wished to capture the essence of the force, to examine it so as to make it reveal to them the powers of understanding. Why?

The artist's challenge is to describe in words, whether written or spoken, the force that changes, molds, and manipulates his world. It is the artist who attempts to freeze time, to offer us answers (and questions), prompting us to think, observe, and live with the world through the medium of the visual form.

For the photographic artist, then, it is even more puzzling. He has within his reach the world and all of its realities as well as all of its forces. And most importantly, he has the ability to hold an instant of it in place for us to thoroughly examine those forces. The viewer thus is allowed time to capture one instant of the world in motion and relate it to his or her own existence. If a scientist can predict the weather (not to mention the future of our earth), then we too can make predictions based upon past aesthetic record.

It is through the photographs of Algimantas Kezys that we can examine this past while being in the present and perhaps we can get a glimpse of the future as well.

The photographs in this book are not cold and isolated calculations. They are graphically sensitive and searching. Kezys's use of the camera as a second eye and his own inner eye teach us a lesson about time and its forces through form. The form, then, appears as a recognizable subject, namely, the land.

Landscape photography usually takes one of two directions for most photographers. Its interpretation can be either documentation or designed intention—abstract, in other words. It can be manipulated before, during, or after in the artistic process. No one of these is more significant than another, for we must remember that we are already at least one step removed from the real world to begin with. We are removed through the lens of the camera and the artist's personal feelings about his subject. The forces he sees attract his attention and fuse with his own inner forces causing a creative reaction—"click" another instant captured.

It would be exciting for us, whether we are scientists or art lovers, to feel we were in control of the examination end of this reaction. For Kezys, and for this collection of photographs, it is important to reveal the forces of nature through both temperaments, showing not only a growth and evolution of the land but also the evolution of his own feelings and personal vision as an artist.

For the purists, people and their environments may not present a proper mix. Ansel Adams would never have dreamed of photographing a person alongside something so grand as nature; if anything, he would have preferred to exclude people altogether. Kezys, on the other hand, prefers an occasional interruption of the natural scene with the inclusion of the force presented by humankind. It is a reckoning force and perhaps it addresses itself to the old quarrel of people trying to conquer their surroundings. In many of the photos we see Kezys introducing a person as a strictly abstract element, no more or no less important than the stone, bark, or dirt beside him. At other times, however, (and later in the chronology), we see the artist allowing the human figure to be at ease with the environment—to just be!—as if the theory of natural selection was put on hold.

It is natural to assume that the artist's religious background is a force we must be aware of here. At times the ethereal quality of the human image can only be seen as an "Adam" type of philosophy. Man walking through the lushest or most barren of landscapes, at peace with serenity or excommunicated from the grandeur. This placement/displacement feeling adds an element of drama to the works.

Certainly for the artist, his Lithuanian childhood finds its way to the surface of the photographs as an attempt to wander and marvel at the riches of a new land. We can imagine ourselves as visitors to a distant land and imagine our own wonderment as we gaze upon the Great Pyramids with the Sahara sweeping up to their bases—a sight we had only before "seen" in picture books. The eye is still fresh, as if the scene were foreign to it; but the eye is sympathetic to the universal qualities that transcend time and image.

Over a twenty-year period of time, the artist Kezys brings to us a changing view of our world, particularly that aspect which has been sought as a wellspring of nature—our parks. These areas, not to be taken lightly, are truly the last vestige of the important terra firma. They are the documents of our past, our present enjoyment, and the graphic keys to our future. To walk through them appreciatively, we must see with the eye of the scientist and the eye of the artist. We must examine up close the forces at work: their abstract tracings on the trees, the ground, the water, and their documented loveliness. We must appreciate both sides of the ecological coin. Algimantas Kezys does so, and through the pages of this book he relates those forces both abstract and documentative in nature for us.

The twenty-year span in which the artist examines and distills the forces of nature presents us with a faithful and uplifting experience. The confirmation of the artist's spirit appears in this dichotomy of science/art relationship with a renaissance-like courage. There is a courageous and artistic honesty which prevails through this artist's faith in growth. He has stated, "1965 was my best year. I was fresh and so was the world. I tend to only want to document it now. It fascinates me—the forces at work, especially on the land."

Kezys's work is exciting. It is a revelation of visual experiment in composition and first-time awareness of a new outlook on the world and how to decipher it. The artist presents to us a legible, transmittable, analytical means which, though focused on ephemeral material, still has its permanent steady force. Kezys, like the French photographer Henri Cartier-Bresson, delivers to us an attitude that is definitely artistic along with his craftsmanship in reporting. This can be found in the ensuing pages and more so in the broad scale of works found in the exhibition which prompted this book (Midwest Museum of American Art, 1985). The philosophy, then, is at once traditional, logical, and exemplary. It is, as Cartier-Bresson described his own approach, "A velvet hand, a hawk's eye . . ."[1]

In summary, this book is about change and the forces which bring it about! Nature as a diagram and an artistic expression. There is a shifting emphasis from abstract form to graphic reality—an artistic searching, not just a leisurely walk—an exercise in self-discovery using the world of nature as a vehicle—twenty years of evolution and transformation. Kezys shows us this evolution in this book through the relationship of two images side by side. In the exhibition it was obvious through the mere scale of the works. The book, then, becomes a personal guide as much as a document.

Photographer Harry Calahan did much to regionalize his vision by using his native environment of Chicago as artistic subject and oftentimes backdrop. He exposed mystery through irony. Kezys merely reverses the process and shows us irony through the mystery of a larger (more Stiechen-like) sensibility—a world of Nature with its forms and forces.

BRIAN BYRN

Curator of Exhibitions
Midwest Museum of American Art

1 *Photographs by Cartier-Bresson*, introduction by Beaumont Newhall. (New York: Grossman Publishers, 1963)

1

Water and Waterfalls

2

Patterns of the Earth

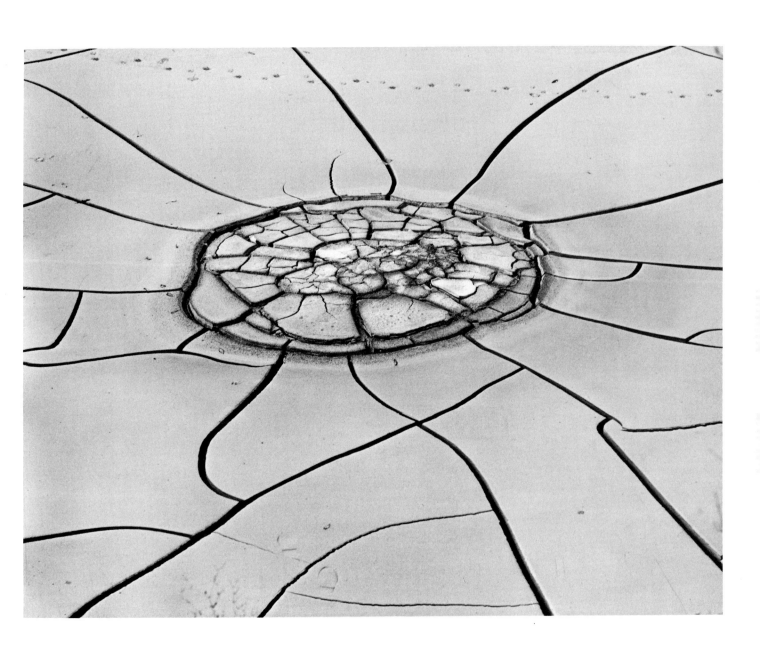

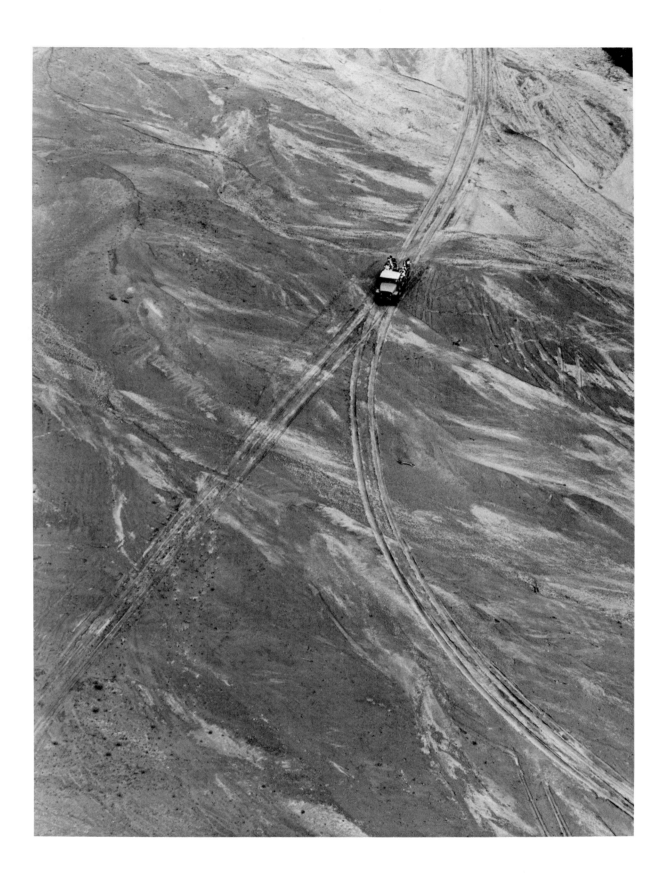

3
Enduring Stone

4

Sand Dunes and Seashores

5
Forms of Trees

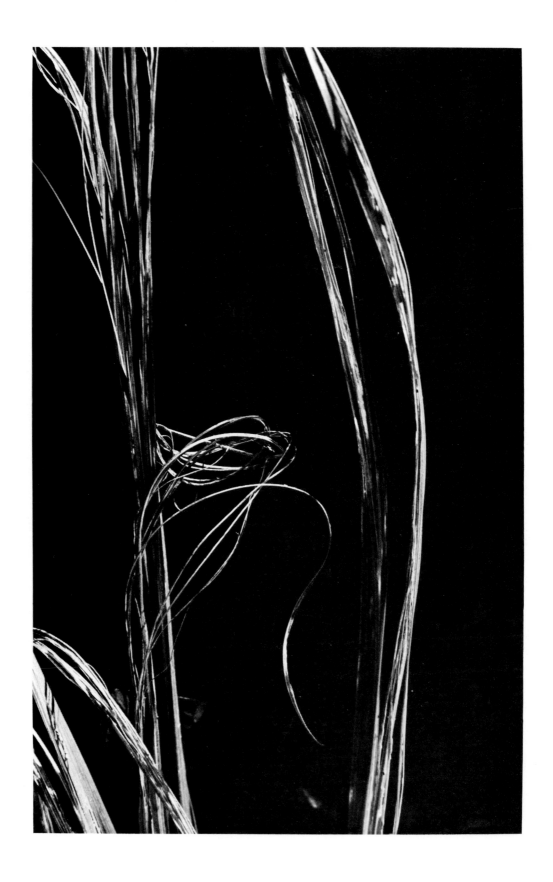

6

Hot Springs of Yellowstone

LIST OF PHOTOGRAPHS

National Bridges State Park; Santa Cruz,
California, 1971   vi

1   Water and Waterfalls

Dam in Evergreen, Colorado, 1971   1
Laurel Falls, Great Smoky Mountains National
Park, Tennessee, 1982   2
Norris Basin, Yellowstone National Park,
Wyoming, 1965   3
Lower Falls, Tahquamenon Falls,
Upper Peninsula, Michigan, 1980   4
Red Canyon, Utah, 1971   5
Tower Falls, Yellowstone National Park,
Wyoming, 1965   6
Grand Canyon of the Yellowstone River,
Yellowstone National Park, Wyoming, 1965   7
Niagara Falls, New York, 1972   8
Upper Falls, Tahquamenon Falls,
Upper Peninsula, Michigan, 1980   9
Niagara Falls, Ontario, Canada, 1972   10
Niagara Falls, New York, 1968   11
Niagara Falls, New York, 1969   12
Niagara Falls, New York, 1969   13

2   Patterns of the Earth

Buffalo Rock State Park, near Ottawa, Illinois,
1968   17
Mud pattern, Buffalo Rock State Park, near
Ottawa, Illinois, 1974   18
Twisted tree stump, Custer National Forest,
Wyoming, 1981   19
Old tree stump, Bistineau Lake State Park,
Louisiana, 1975   20
Cracked mud, Buffalo Rock State Park, near
Ottawa, Illinois, 1975   21
Badlands National Park, South Dakota, 1965   22
Badlands National Park, South Dakota, 1965   23
Buffalo Rock State Park, near Ottawa, Illinois,
1974   24
Coal mines, Shenandoah, Pennsylvania, 1973   25
Dry stream bed, Canyon de Chelly, Arizona,
1970   26
Buffalo Rock State Park, near Ottawa, Illinois,
1968   27
Theodore Roosevelt National Park, Badlands,
North Dakota, 1981   28
Meramec Caverns, Stanton, Missouri, 1969   29
Theodore Roosevelt National Park, Badlands,
North Dakota, 1981   30
Theodore Roosevelt National Park, Badlands,
North Dakota, 1981   31

3 Enduring Stone

Natural Chimneys, Mt. Solon, Virginia, 1971 — 35
Castle Rock, St. Ignace, Michigan, 1980 — 36
Ship Rock, near Coloma, Michigan, 1980 — 37
Lover's Leap, Calaway Gardens, near West Point Pine Mountains, Georgia, 1975 — 28
Pompey's Pillar, National Historic Landmark, near Billings, Montana, 1981 — 39
Grand Canyon National Park, Arizona, 1965 — 40
Bryce Canyon National Park, Utah, 1965 — 41
Bryce Canyon National Park, Utah, 1965 — 42
Bryce Canyon National Park, Utah, 1965 — 43
Banks of the Yellowstone River, Yellowstone National Park, Wyoming, 1965 — 44
Path carved in rock, Canyon de Chelly, Arizona, 1970 — 45
Wupatki National Monument, near Flagstaff, Arizona, 1971 — 46
Cliff dwellings, Mesa Verde National Park, Colorado, 1965 — 47

4 Sand Dunes and Seashores

Beach, Santa Cruz, California, 1971 — 51
Sand dunes, near Parker Dam, Arizona, 1971 — 52
Sand dunes, near Parker Dam, Arizona, 1971 — 53
Silver Lake State Park, Michigan, 1972 — 54
Silver Lake State Park, Michigan, 1975 — 55
Silver Lake State Park, Michigan, 1976 — 56
Devil's Lake State Park, Wisconsin, 1973 — 57
Beach, Santa Cruz, California, 1971 — 58
Reservoir, East Canyon State Park, Utah, 1971 — 59
Cape Cod Beach, Provincetown, Massachusetts, 1978 — 60
Beach, Marco Island, Florida, 1983 — 61
San Mateo County Memorial Park, near La Honda, California, 1971 — 62
Gunnison River Reservoir, near Gunnison, Colorado, 1970 — 63

5 Forms of Trees

Mald Botanical Gardens, Orlando, Florida, 1970 — 67
San Juan Capistrano Mission, San Juan Capistrano, California, 1966 — 68
Huntington Botanical Gardens, San Marino, California, 1973 — 69
Trees along Highway 98, Florida, 1970 — 70
Mammoth Cave National Park, Kentucky, 1974 — 71
McKee Jungle Gardens, Vero Beach, Florida, 1970 — 72
Hugh Taylor Birch State Park, Fort Lauderdale, Florida, 1968 — 73
Joshua Tree National Monument, California, 1971 — 74
Disneyland, Disneyland, California, 1974 — 75
Norris Geyser Basin, Yellowstone National Park, Wyoming, 1981 — 76
Hot Springs National Park, Hot Springs, Arkansas, 1984 — 77
Plant, Los Angeles, California, 1974 — 78
Alfred B. Maclay State Gardens, Tallahassee, Florida, 1974 — 79
Buena Vista's Exotic Animal Paradise, Springfield, Missouri, 1972 — 80
Bistineau Lake State Park, Louisiana, 1975 — 81
Road to Mountain Tower, Hot Springs National Park, Arkansas, 1984 — 82
Rosedown Plantation and Gardens, St. Francisville, Louisiana, 1976 — 83
Jungle Gardens, Avery Island, Louisiana, 1976 — 84
Jungle Gardens, Avery Island, Louisiana, 1976 — 85
Tree roots, Lower Tahquamenon Falls, Upper Peninsula, Michigan, 1980 — 86
Huntington Botanical Gardens, San Marino, California, 1973 — 87
Humboldt Redwoods State Park, California, 1966 — 88

Great Smoky Mountains National Park,
    Tennessee, 1982   89
Mississippi River, near St. Louis, Missouri, 1969   90
Wisconsin State Park, near Beloit, Wisconsin,
    1976   91

6   Hot Springs of Yellowstone

Fountain Paint Pot, Yellowstone National
    Park, Wyoming, 1965   95
Mammoth Hot Springs, Yellowstone National
    Park, Wyoming, 1965   96
Mammoth Hot Springs, Yellowstone National
    Park, Wyoming, 1965   97
Mammoth Hot Springs, Yellowstone National
    Park, Wyoming, 1965   98
Mammoth Hot Springs, Yellowstone National
    Park, Wyoming, 1966   99
Mammoth Hot Springs, Yellowstone National
    Park, Wyoming, 1965   100

Mammoth Hot Springs, Yellowstone National
    Park, Wyoming, 1965   101
Mammoth Hot Springs, Yellowstone National
    Park, Wyoming, 1965   102
Mammoth Hot Springs, Yellowstone National
    Park, Wyoming, 1966   103
Soda Butte Cone, Yellowstone National Park,
    Wyoming, 1965   104
Paintpot Fountain, Yellowstone National Park,
    Wyoming, 1981   105
Isa Lake, Yellowstone National Park, Wyoming,
    1965   106
Isa Lake, Yellowstone National Park, Wyoming,
    1965   107
Midway Geyser Basin, Yellowstone National
    Park, Wyoming, 1981   108
Midway Geyser Basin, Yellowstone National
    Park, Wyoming, 1965   109
Norris Geyser Basin, Yellowstone National
    Park, Wyoming, 1965   110